INVESTIGATING THE SUPERNATURAL

Heinemann
LIBRARY

. . . . . PAUL MASON . . . . .

www.heinemann.co.uk/library
Visit our website to find out more information about Heinemann Library books.

To order:
 Phone 44 (0) 1865 888066
 Send a fax to 44 (0) 1865 314091
 Visit the Heinemann Bookshop at www.heinemann.co.uk/library to browse our catalogue and order online.

First published in Great Britain by Heinemann Library, Halley Court, Jordan Hill, Oxford OX2 8EJ, part of Harcourt Education. Heinemann is a registered trademark of Harcourt Education Ltd.

© Harcourt Education Ltd 2004
The moral right of the proprietor has been asserted.

Editorial: Sarah Eason, Georga Godwin and Kate Bellamy
Design: Jo Hinton-Malivoire and AMR
Picture Research: Rosie Garai and Andrea Sadler
Production: Edward Moore

Originated by Ambassador Litho Ltd
Printed and bound in China by South China Printing Company
The paper used to print this book comes from sustainable resources

ISBN 0 431 16024 4
08 07 06 05 04
10 9 8 7 6 5 4 3 2 1

British Library Cataloguing in Publication Data

Mason, Paul
Investigating the Supernatural
133
A full catalogue record for this book is available from the British Library.

Acknowledgements

The Publishers would like to thank the following for permission to reproduce photographs:
Alpine Club Photo Library, London p. **24**; Bridgeman Art Library/Peasbody & Essex Museum p. **12**; Bruce Schmidt/www.ZurichMansion.org pp. **35**, **36**; Charles Tait pp. **28**, **29**; Fortean Picture Library pp. **14**, **15**, **20**, **23**, **26**, **38**; Fortean Picture Library p. **19** (John Sibbick), p. **5** (Guy Lyon) Playfair; Frank Spooner Pictures/Gamma p. **16** (L. Vanderstockt); Getty Images/Stone p. **40**; Holt Studios p. **11**; Hulton Archive p. **42**; Katz p. **33**; Mary Evans Picture Library p. **30**; Michael Hogan p. **18**; popperfoto.com p. **41**; Rex Features/Sipa Press p. **32**; Royal Geographic Society p. **25**; Salem Witch Trials Museum p. **8**; Science Photo Library p. **27** (Roger Harris); Stockphoto.com p. **7** (Richard Flaco).

Cover photograph of ghostly figure reproduced with permission of Stone/Getty.

The Publishers would like to thank Peter Bull and Nicola Greene for their assistance in the preparation of this book.

Disclaimer

Contents

Any words appearing in the text in bold, **like this**, are explained in the Glossary.

Supernatural investigation

The story starts in 1984, when a short article is published in a newspaper in a small town in the USA. This article describes strange events that seem to centre on a fourteen-year-old girl. Her family has been scared by loud noises that cannot be explained. Furniture has moved around, apparently without any human help. Lamps have toppled over on their own, and small objects have flown through the air without anyone picking them up and throwing them. No one can explain how these things are happening – after all, science tells us that furniture cannot move unless someone or something moves it.

Sensational news

Sensing a popular story, reporters from other newspapers pay visits. So do TV crews, first from local stations, then from national ones. Many of the journalists **witness** the same strange events, and for a while the story reaches the top of the news agenda. People around the world are fascinated to hear the next instalment of the story of the **supernatural** events in the small American town.

The story gets an added twist when it emerges that the girl at its centre is an **adopted** child. She is desperate to meet her real parents, and the media attention allows her to launch an appeal for them to get in contact with her. The added interest of her search means that more TV crews arrive.

Caught on camera

Then one of the TV cameras is left on by accident. The camera records the girl pulling over a lamp and moving a piece of furniture. She calls people into the room, and claims to have been asleep and woken by the lamp falling over. On waking up, she says, she discovered that the furniture had moved on its own. But the camera tells the truth: the whole thing is a **hoax**. The TV crew finishes with one final story – about how the whole thing was made up by an unhappy young adopted girl trying to locate her birth parents. Like many apparently supernatural events, this one has been discovered to be rooted in the ordinary world.

This furniture was apparently slashed by a **poltergeist** in Brazil in 1973.

The supernatural world

The subjects that can be included under the heading 'supernatural' are very varied. Among them are:

- Hauntings — where spirits make themselves known to people. Sometimes these spirits are visible and look like the shape of a human being. Other spirits are invisible, but make their presence known through noises or by moving things around.

- Black magic — an evil type of **witchcraft**, where the enemies of Christianity are said to make alliances with the Devil in return for special supernatural powers.

- Supernatural creatures — including giant cats, lake monsters and the *chupacabra* [Goatsucker].

- Shape-shifting humans — for example, werewolves and vampires.

Scientific investigations

Scientific investigations

Something that is **supernatural** is something that operates beyond the laws of nature. At least, we cannot explain it using our understanding of how the natural world works. So, what part can science play in investigating supernatural events? After all, science is about discovering, verifying and stating how we think the world works. Through science, we 'know', for example, that a young girl lying in bed cannot simply start to rise up into the air. Yet there are many reports of such events.

Scientific answers

Science can often provide an **explanation** for events that appear to be supernatural but are not. These may be things that genuinely mystify everyone, and apparently have no chance of being explained. But then some crucial piece of information comes to light, which allows scientists to show what actually happened.

Scientific working methods

Recording what happens and then trying to offer an explanation for it also has a part to play in supernatural **investigations**. Many people attempting to put together a **hoax** have been uncovered because **investigators** were determined to record everything that happened.

Poltergeists

A **poltergeist** is a ghost that throws things around, knocks objects over and generally causes damage to its surroundings.

Poltergeists usually turn up in the homes of unhappy adolescents, and their activities take place only when that person is there. If the cause of the unhappiness disappears, the poltergeist usually leaves, too. No one has ever proved that the link between teenagers and poltergeists is supernatural.

Investigating the supernatural

The elements in a supernatural investigator's toolbox include:

- Cameras, both video and still — investigations into hauntings have often ended when a hidden camera catches someone faking **evidence**.

- **Voice analysis** — analysing a voice heard on a tape can sometimes show who was speaking. Scientific instruments can indicate volume, pitch and other variables. All these are used to help to identify the speaker.

- Scientific research — it is possible to find a scientific explanation for events through the development of new knowledge. For example, **Kirlian photography** was thought to measure a person's 'life force'. But scientists now know that the differences found in Kirlian photos are due to changes in air pressure, humidity and electrical conductivity, and not to do with a life force.

- Gauss meters — for measuring the strength of electromagnetic fields.

- Geiger counters — to check levels of radiation.

- **Magnetic field** detectors — to check for unusually strong magnetic signals.

- Tremolo meters — to analyse the level of stress in someone's voice.

An investigator of the supernatural at work.

The witches of Salem

(Question) 'What evil spirit have you familiarity with?'
(Answer)   'None.'
(Q) 'Have you made no contract with the devil?'
(A) 'No.'
(Q) 'Why do you hurt these children?'
(A) 'I do not hurt them. I scorn it.'
(Q) 'Who do you employ then to do it?'
(A) 'I employ nobody.'
(Q) 'What creature do you employ then?'
(A) 'No creature. I am falsely **accused**.'

These words were spoken in New England, America, in 1692. Two **magistrates**, John Hathorne and Jonathan Corwin, were questioning a woman named Sarah Good. Good had been accused of **witchcraft** – a serious crime, as a convicted witch could be hanged. Good was found guilty, and was hanged for witchcraft on 19 July 1692.

A memorial for one of the eighteen Salem 'witches' who were hanged as punishment for their 'crime'.

Sarah Good was not the only person to be executed as a witch – between 10 June and 22 September 1692, thirteen women and five men were hanged. Seventeen others died in prison, and one man was crushed to death for refusing to take part in a trial. All these events took place around Salem village, and the events are now known as the Salem Witch trials.

Strange behaviour

The events began in January 1692. The daughter and niece of Reverend Samuel Parris became ill and started to behave strangely. They would shout and scream, go into a curious **trance**-like state, have **convulsions** and speak against God. Soon afterwards, other girls from the village began to have the same problems. The village doctor, William Griggs, was unable to identify any disease that they could be suffering from. He said that the girls were bewitched – under the influence of the Devil.

Aggravating factors

In the early days of the Salem Witch trials, a number of factors added to the atmosphere of confusion and panic in Salem:

- Semi-starvation, caused by the communal **fasting** led by Reverend Parris. People who have not eaten for some time become feverish and lose their ability to make good decisions.

- Cotton Mather, a Boston preacher, and his father, Increase Mather, were influential figures who convinced the people that there were witches at work.

- Sleep deprivation, from long prayer meetings, late nights and early mornings. This also stops people making good decisions.

- Salem had recently suffered an outbreak of the killer disease smallpox, leaving some people weak and more likely to suffer the worst effects of starvation and sleep deprivation.

- The villagers also feared attack by local Native American tribes, which made them feel persecuted and afraid.

Religious beliefs

In New England in the 17th century, this was a serious situation. Most people had stronger religious beliefs than we do today. They thought that the Devil was a real presence trying to tempt them away from Christianity.

By late February 1692, Reverend Parris was conducting prayer services and organizing community fasting, hoping that the evil forces would be discouraged by this show of Christian determination.

Desperate people

The people of Salem were desperate to root out the Devil and his followers. A man named John Indian baked a 'witch cake', made of rye grain mixed with urine (wee) from an **afflicted** girl. The witch cakes were fed to an animal. If the animal started to twitch and have convulsions, this confirmed that the girl was, indeed, bewitched.

Pressure was also put on the afflicted girls to identify their tormentors. They named three women: Sarah Good, Sarah Osborne and Tituba, the Reverend Parris's Native American slave. Good and Osborne denied being witches, but Tituba admitted that she met with the Devil, who she said was 'sometimes like a hog and sometimes like a great dog'. Tituba also told the **investigators** that she was not alone – there was a conspiracy of witches in Salem.

God and the Devil

This idea sent shockwaves through the community, but in a way it also fitted in with what people expected. The people of Salem would largely have seen life in religious terms, as a battle between God and the Devil. What was more natural than that the Devil, having decided to go to work in Salem, should recruit a network of witches to help him?

Harmful spectres

Very quickly, the atmosphere in Salem Village became strained. **Accusations** and counter-accusations went back and forth. Many people came forward to tell the two investigating magistrates that they had been harmed by the **spectres** of witches, for example, by having fits or sickness. At the time, witches were thought to be able to use spectres to do their work. A spectre was the ghost-like form of a witch, invisible to everyone except the witch's victim, and therefore impossible to disprove.

Ergot poisoning

A key question about the Salem Witch trials is why the young women began to have fits and convulsions in the first place. One of the prime candidates is a fungus called ergot. Ergot is a parasitic fungus that grows on wheat, barley, rye and many grasses. Most commonly, it attacks rye, which was one of the common foods in 17th century New England.

Eating rye with the ergot fungus in it can cause a number of health problems, among them convulsions. Ergot can also affect people's minds. One of the most powerful **hallucinogenic** drugs, **LSD**, was first made from ergot in 1938. LSD can lead people to feel anxious, confused or scared, and to think that imaginary **visions** are real.

It is worth remembering that the witch cakes used in Salem to try to root out witches were also made with rye grain. If this grain contained ergot, it could well have led to the girls' strange behaviour, 'proving' that they were witches.

The ergot fungus can be seen here, growing out of some ears of wheat.

Witchcraft trials

In the rising panic, a special court was set up and seven judges were appointed. These judges based their decisions on various things that, today, would not be considered proof. The key element of the witchcraft trials was that the judges took notice of 'spectral **evidence**'.

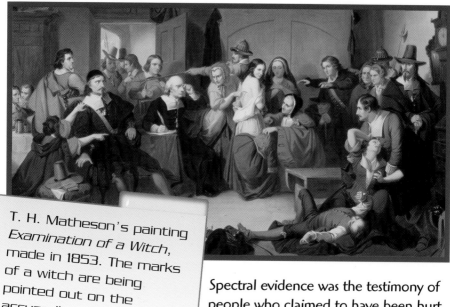

T. H. Matheson's painting *Examination of a Witch*, made in 1853. The marks of a witch are being pointed out on the accused's back.

Spectral evidence was the testimony of people who claimed to have been hurt by the 'spectres' of witches. The problem with this was that a witch's spectre was believed to be invisible to anybody except its victim. The only 'proof' that the spectre existed was the word of the person doing the accusing.

Accusations

There were many possible reasons for alleging that someone was a witch, and not just genuinely thinking that they were one. Personal dislike, jealousy, business rivalry (competition) or religious arguments could all have led one person to accuse another of being a witch.

Guilty

In this situation, the courts found thirteen women and five men guilty of witchcraft. Each of them was hanged and their bodies were refused burial in the churchyard. A further seventeen accused witches died in prison, among them Sarah Osborne, one of the first women to be accused.

SOLVED

Bridget Bishop was the first person to be hanged for witchcraft. When she died, several of the villagers signed a petition saying that they believed some of those accused to be innocent. It did no good.

The trials end

The Salem Witch trials finally ended when the Governor of the colony of Massachusetts, William Phips, dissolved the court. His decision to do this was influenced by a letter written by a man named Thomas Brattle, who criticized the trials. The Governor may also have been helped to make his decision by the fact that his own wife had recently been accused of witchcraft. Whatever the reason, a new Superior Court was set up to hear charges of witchcraft. This new court met in May 1693 but, this time, it did not accept spectral evidence. There were no further convictions, and those who were waiting in prison were released. The Salem Witch trials were over.

Hysteria

Part of the **explanation** for what happened in Salem may have been **psychological**.

The girls who were originally 'afflicted' by witches may have been suffering from a form of **hysteria**. This is a mental illness which causes sufferers to behave wildly. They may also have physical problems, such as vomiting or headaches, even though there is nothing physically wrong with them.

The people of Salem may have been suffering from some sort of mass hysteria, and may have made decisions that they would normally have regarded as unreasonable. Mass hysteria is thought to occur most commonly when a group of people is under a lot of stress — as the villagers of Salem were at the time of the witchcraft trials.

FILE CLOSED

13

On a cold day during the 1700s, a group of people gathered around the grave of a man named Peter Plogojowitz. They were there to dig up his dead body. When he was uncovered, the crowd was stunned. One account of what they saw reported that:

'The hair and beard – even the nails, of which the old ones had fallen away – had grown on the corpse; the old skin, which was somewhat whitish, had peeled away, and a new fresh one had emerged underneath it ... Not without astonishment, I saw some fresh blood in his mouth, which, according to the common observation, he had sucked from the people killed by him.'

These signs convinced the crowd that Plogojowitz was a vampire, a dead person who comes back to life and then survives by drinking the blood of the living.

Origins

The origins of the vampire story are unknown today. One of the people who certainly contributed to the growth of the story was a noblewoman named Elizabeth Bathory, who lived in Transylvania in the 16th century. Bathory was terrified of growing old, and believed that she could keep her skin youthful by bathing it in blood. She imprisoned young servant girls and used terrible torture to make them bleed. Before she was arrested and tried, Bathory is said to have killed more than 600 people.

Elizabeth Bathory, whose bloodthirsty murders of young girls led to the suggestion that she was a vampire.

Count Dracula

Another story that led to the growth of the vampire myth was Bram Stoker's novel *Dracula*. In the novel, the central figure is a Transylvanian count named Dracula. He is a vampire who, having bled dry the country near his home, travels to England in search of fresh blood. Many elements of the modern vampire myth came together in the character of Dracula. The count cannot stand sunlight, and spends the daylight hours sleeping on soil brought from his native land. His victims become vampires themselves once they are dead. The count can change himself into a bat to travel around, or even into a pale smoke so he can pass under doors. He has to be invited into a building before he can enter it.

Vlad Dracul, the historical figure who was part of the inspiration for Bram Stoker's vampire, Dracula.

Porphyria

One **explanation** for vampirism is that the vampires were actually people who were suffering from porphyria. The connection probably stems from the fact that some forms of porphyria cause people to become sensitive to sunlight — so, like vampires, they avoid the light.

Porphyria is a **genetic** condition that occasionally leads people to behave as though they are mad. In fact, sufferers are experiencing a chemical imbalance that affects their behaviour.

The theory goes that people with porphyria drink blood in an attempt to cure their disease, the causes of which are related to the production of heme, one of the things that make up blood. There is no **evidence** to support this idea, however, and there is no evidence to show that drinking blood would be a cure for porphyria.

The myth explained

The signs found on Peter Plogojowitz's dead body were typical of those found on the bodies of many people who were thought to be vampires. Could they be proof that such creatures really do exist?

Physical changes

'The hair and beard ... had grown on the corpse,' reported the witness to Plogojowitz's exhumation (being dug up). The hair and beard of a corpse cannot grow after death, but they can appear to. What actually happens is that the skin on the corpse shrinks, making the hair and the beard stick out further than they used to – giving the appearance that they have grown.

The South American vampire bat is named after the old European vampire stories. Until the time of these stories, bats had not been associated with vampires.

SOLVED

The witnesses also saw that: 'The nails ... had fallen away' and new ones had grown. Nails do fall off when a body **decomposes**; there is nothing surprising about this. In ancient Egypt, mummies had their nails tied on, or had thimbles put over their fingers and toes to stop the nails dropping off. The 'new nails' were probably the old nail bed, which had been exposed.

Most amazingly, 'The old skin had peeled away, and a new fresh one emerged underneath it.' This is actually something that **forensic pathologists** call 'skin slippage', whereby the epidermis (outer layer of skin) flakes away from the dermis (the inner layer of skin).

Finally, the account says there was some 'fresh blood in his mouth that ... he had sucked from the people killed by him'. Fresh blood is not especially unusual in dead bodies. As a human body decomposes, it produces gases. These gases put pressure on the lungs, which can have blood in them. This blood is forced out of the mouth and nose.

These modern scientific explanations were not available to people in the 18th century, so it is not surprising that they invented a **supernatural** creature like a vampire instead. What is surprising is that now we do have scientific explanations, some people continue to believe in vampires.

Corpses that cry out

Legend says that one way to kill a vampire is to drive a wooden stake through its heart. One of the 'proofs' that a dead body is a vampire is said to be that the body cries out one final time when this is done.

In fact, the body, especially the lungs, is filled with gases caused by decomposition. As a stake is driven against the chest cavity, these gases are forced out through the airways and past the glottis (space in the body's windpipe). This makes a noise, but it doesn't prove that the body is still alive, or that it is a vampire.

FILE CLOSED

Legend says that, since 1735, a terrifying creature known as the Jersey Devil has haunted the wild, desolate area known as the Pine Barrens of New Jersey, USA. Witnesses say that the Jersey Devil is about 1.2 metres (4 feet) tall, with a huge head shaped like a horse's head. It has yellow teeth and a pair of horns sticking out of its forehead, and is able to fly using a pair of small wings on its back. It usually appears out of the bleak landscape of the Barrens at night. It attacks livestock, tramples about on people's roofs and appears at their windows. The Jersey Devil is even said to try to snatch small children if the opportunity arises.

Where did it come from?

There are several stories about where the Jersey Devil came from. All agree that it was the child of a woman named Mrs Leeds (the creature is sometimes called the Leeds Devil). Mrs Leeds had twelve children, and was horrified to get pregnant again. 'I don't want another child: let it be a devil!' she exclaimed. When the child was born, it was horrible to look at; it crawled up the chimney and fled. In some versions of the story, the Jersey Devil stopped to eat its brothers and sisters before leaving; in others, the midwife died of shock when it appeared.

Pine Barrens is in a lonely and wild part of New Jersey.

Why was it born?

Some versions of the story say that Mrs Leeds gave birth to the Devil because she had angered a priest; others claim that a gypsy's curse was responsible. One story even says that the Devil was a punishment on Mrs Leeds because its father was not her husband but a British soldier

Whatever the truth of its origins, the Jersey Devil haunted the Pine Barrens for the next five years, eating livestock and small children to stay alive. Finally, the legend says that in about 1740 a priest **exorcized** the Jersey Devil, sending it away for the next 90 years.

The next time the Jersey Devil was seen was during the 1830s and 1840s. The first documented accounts of the Jersey Devil date from about 1859, with further reports appearing in 1873 and 1880.

Chupacabra

The Jersey Devil is very similar to the *chupacabra* from Latin America. The *chupacabra* is also called the Goatsucker, because it attacks goats and sheep and drinks their blood. It is described as 'a fanged, kangaroo-like entity with bulging red eyes' and, like the Jersey Devil, it usually appears at night. Some people believe that the *chupacabra* can fly.

Often, people from a particular place take their stories about **supernatural** creatures with them when they move to another place. But when the Jersey Devil first appeared, people from Latin America had not moved to the Pine Barrens of New Jersey. Because of this, the two creatures appear to be different, even though the stories of many witnesses say that they look very alike.

The *chupacabra* drinks the blood of a goat. Might this be a distant relative of the Jersey Devil?

Sightings

One of the earliest properly recorded sightings of the Jersey Devil was reported in a small Philadelphia newspaper in 1899. A loud, high-pitched screaming outside his house apparently woke a local businessman called George Saarosy. He got out of bed and pulled back the curtains – just in time to see the Jersey Devil fly past his window.

In 1909, the *Philadelphia Record* reported a rampage of Jersey Devil activity that peaked in the week of 16–23 January. More than 1000 people reported that their animals had been killed, strange noises had been heard at night and mysterious hoof marks had appeared around their homes. Also, several policemen reported taking shots at it.

Reward offered

Many people found the Jersey Devil sightings laughable. Even the Philadelphia Zoo joined in, offering a $10,000 reward to anyone who could capture it. The reward was intended as a joke, but then word arrived in Philadelphia that the Jersey Devil had been captured.

The *Philadelphia Evening Bulletin*'s impression of the Jersey Devil shows a curiously comical creature.

SOLVED

Norman Jefferies and Jacob Hope claimed to have caught the Jersey Devil together. But when **investigators** examined the creature's body, they found that the 'Devil' was actually a kangaroo, on to which Jefferies and Hope had glued claws and a pair of wings. The reward went unclaimed.

Despite this **hoax**, further reports of the Jersey Devil continued. In 1951, a young boy apparently saw a creature with 'blood dripping from its face' at his bedroom window, sparking a rash of sightings. Then, in 1961, a farmer lost a whole barn full of animals to the Jersey Devil, including two fierce German Shepherd dogs. Like the other animals, the dogs had been ripped apart. Scattered reports of the Jersey Devil have continued into the 21st century.

Devil or hoax?

No one has been able to prove that the Jersey Devil *doesn't* exist — but that is not the same as saying that it *does* exist. Most sightings have turned out to be hoaxes or mistaken identity:

- In the 250 or so years since the story was first told, no one has ever captured the Jersey Devil, or even taken a photo of it.

- The only captured 'Jersey Devil', in 1909, turned out to be a kangaroo with glued-on wings.

- Police investigating sightings of the Jersey Devil in 1951 followed its tracks, only to find a stick with a stuffed bear's paw attached to it.

- More recent sightings have been of a creature about 1.8 metres (6 feet) tall, likely to have been a man named George Bishop, who lived wild in the woods. One local remembers: 'He would freak people out when they saw him. George used to love hearing about people seeing him and swearing they saw the Jersey Devil.'

FILE CLOSED

From the depths of the frozen English winter of 1855 comes a famous **supernatural** mystery. Strange events and physical proof caused the people of a quiet corner of the country to believe in a supernatural event. Had their neighbourhood been visited by the Devil on one frozen night?

A trail of prints

On the morning of 8 February 1855, Alfred Brailsford opened his front door in Topsham, Devon, to one of the coldest days of the year. Snow lay on the ground, which was unusual for a place that normally has a warm climate. Brailsford, the headmaster of the local school, noticed a curious sight. Running down the middle of the snowy street was a line of what looked like footprints or hoof prints. They ran dead straight, one in front of the other, with a gap of about 8 inches between them. The tracks appeared to be 'branded' into the snow, fixed there solidly. Rather than looking like squashed snow, they seemed to be cast in ice.

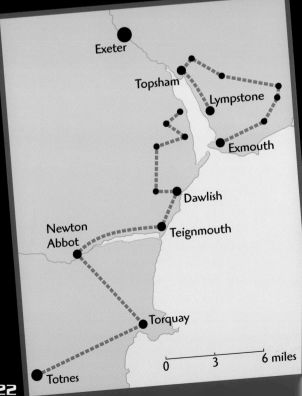

Soon, Brailsford and other men from the village were following the trail of prints, but they were stopped when the prints ended at a brick wall. Then someone noticed that the tracks continued on the other side of the wall, even though the snow on top was undisturbed.

The Devil's footprints wandered across the Devon countryside for roughly 65 kilometres (40 miles).

The trail of prints wandered through a large number of towns and villages from Lympstone to Totnes. All in all it covered about 65 kilometres (40 miles) and, at one point, whatever made the prints seemed to have crossed the River Exe. There was no **evidence** of anyone having made the tracks as a **hoax**, because there were no other impressions in the snow except for the prints. The mysterious nature of the trail – added to the fact that in places the prints looked as though they had been made by a **cloven hoof** – led people to fear that they had been made by the Devil himself.

A possible explanation

It took many years for the likely true **explanation** to emerge. A local man named Major Carter told **investigators** in the 1980s that one of his relatives had worked in Devonport dockyard, which is very close to Topham, at the time the Devil's footprints appeared. On the night of 7 February 1855 a balloon had escaped its moorings inside the military base, and dragged off across country. Major Carter's grandfather remembered the incident being hushed up because the balloon had damaged several pieces of property before being recaptured. Trailing lines or other equipment from the balloon could have made prints in the snow, and their shape could have been distorted in the morning light.

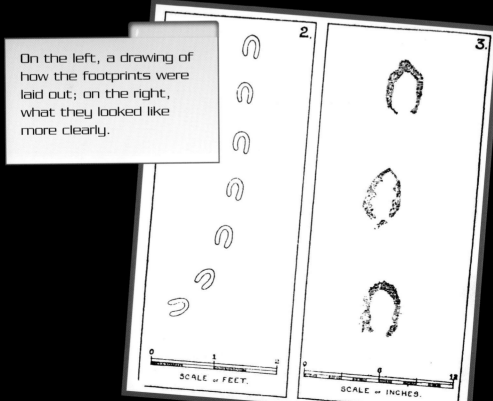

On the left, a drawing of how the footprints were laid out; on the right, what they looked like more clearly.

The Grey Man of Ben Macdhui

In 1890 a well-known **mountaineer**, Professor Norman Collie, was climbing on the Scottish mountain Ben Macdhui. The mountain stands at the heart of the Cairngorm range, 1300 metres (4260 feet) above the valley of the River Spey. It is a remote setting, and Collie was climbing there alone. But as he headed down from the **summit cairn** through heavy mist, Collie heard noises among the rocks behind him. He later said it seemed 'as if someone was walking after me, but taking steps three or four times the length of my own'. Feeling distinctly worried, Collie continued to descend carefully. Suddenly, though, he was 'seized with terror and took to my heels', feeling he was being pursued by the mysterious presence. The professor didn't stop running until he had reached the safety of Rothiemurchus Forest, 6.5 kilometres (4 miles) away.

Strange happenings

The mountain has had a frightening reputation for many years. Other climbers have had mysterious experiences on Ben Macdhui. Some have simply felt a terrifying presence; others have actually seen a strange man-like creature on the mountainside. Often, this creature is called the Big Grey Man, for it stands as much as 6 metres (20 feet) tall. Its **Gaelic** name is Fear Liath More.

The mountaineer Norman Collie and other members of his mountaineering club.

One strange story concerns a mountaineer who refused to believe in the Grey Man, and agreed to camp near the summit cairn for a bet. He pitched his tent one night in January, but soon began to feel nervous for no apparent reason. However, the climber managed to fall asleep. Later that night, he woke feeling **petrified**. Looking out of a narrow crack in the entrance to his tent, he

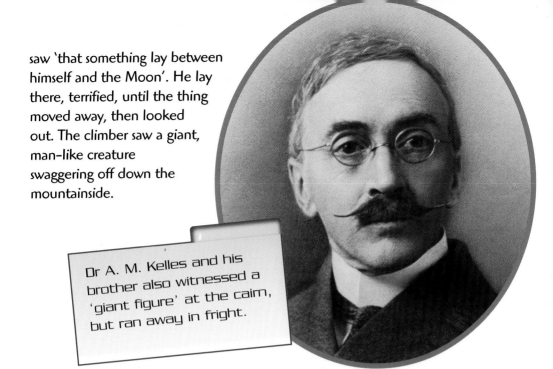

saw 'that something lay between himself and the Moon'. He lay there, terrified, until the thing moved away, then looked out. The climber saw a giant, man-like creature swaggering off down the mountainside.

Dr A. M. Kelles and his brother also witnessed a 'giant figure' at the cairn, but ran away in fright.

Panic sites

There seem to be some places in the world that cause certain people to panic. These places are often in isolated spots, where the natural world rules and modern developments are far away. On Ben Macdhui, many climbers have reported mysterious feelings of panic. The writer John Buchan was walking in the Bavarian Alps when he and his companion suddenly became so scared that they ran all the way to the valley floor, miles below.

The Cambridge academic Tom Lethbridge and his wife were once gripped by an irrational depression at the base of a cliff at Ladram beach in Devon. In the end, his wife Mina said that she couldn't 'stand this place any longer', and complained, 'There's something frightful here.' Lethbridge noted that it was possible to enter and leave the feeling with one step: it seemed to have an exact boundary. In the meantime, Mina had walked to the top of the cliff, only to feel that she was being urged to jump off. They later discovered that someone had committed suicide at that exact spot.

A harmful will

Sometimes the 'presence' on Ben Macdhui seems to wish people harm. A well-known climber called Peter Densham was in charge of aeroplane rescue work in the Cairngorms during the Second World War. Densham told a story of how he had climbed up to the summit cairn one day and sat down to eat some chocolate. Suddenly, the mist closed in and strange noises began to ring out. He felt something was nearby in the mist, and went to see what it was. Almost immediately, he was gripped by a feeling of terror, and found himself running towards Lurcher's Crag. Had he kept going he would have run off a sheer cliff. 'It was as if someone was pushing me,' Densham said. 'I managed to deflect my course, but only with a great degree of difficulty.'

This 1917 illustration of a 'wild man' in Scotland may have been inspired by the Grey Man.

Ambush site

It has been suggested that the presence on Ben Macdhui is a shadow or echo of terrible past events. Some places are said to have a 'memory' of events that have happened there. The mountaineer Frank Smythe described once how he had been walking in the hills when he wandered into a grassy gap in the high ground. Suddenly, he felt that 'something terrible had happened there, and time had failed to dissipate [break up or remove] the atmosphere created by it'.

Smythe decided to eat his lunch on the grass and, as he sat there, the feeling grew stronger. Then he seemed to see a **vision** of an ambush in which about twenty people were **massacred**. He later discovered that the spot had been the site of an ambush, where British troops had massacred a group of Highlanders. But Smythe thought the events he'd seen dated from an earlier time. Possibly, the site had been the location of two massacres. However, no past event on Ben Macdhui has been identified that could have caused the feeling of dread that seems to haunt the mountain.

Magnetic forces

One possible **explanation** for the events on Ben Macdhui is that it could be a place where the Earth's **magnetic field** is sometimes especially strong. It could be that this strong magnetism — sometimes associated with large areas of rock — has an effect on people's brains.

People may subconsciously sense that something is unusual nearby, triggering an automatic response that tells them to flee. Some people may be more sensitive to this magnetic force than others, which would explain why not everyone is affected.

There is no real scientific proof of this theory at the moment. However, recent studies by a Canadian scientist named Michael Persinger have shown that people's feelings can be affected by magnetism. Up to 80 per cent of the people he tested found that, when an artificial magnetic field was focused on certain parts of their brain, it made them feel as if someone was with them — even if they were alone.

The Earth's magnetic field. Magnetism has been shown to affect how people feel.

The mystery of Eilean More

Just a few days before Christmas 1900, the tiny Scottish island of Eilean More was home to a mystery that it seemed impossible to solve. The light of the island's lighthouse suddenly went out. When a ship was sent to find out what had happened, an even bigger mystery was discovered. All three lighthouse keepers had disappeared.

The lighthouse on the island of Eilean More.

On the night of 15 December 1900, word reached the Northern Lighthouse Board that the lamp on Eilean More had not been lit. The Board sent Joseph Moore to investigate but, the next day, the seas were too stormy for a ship to be launched. In the end, it wasn't until 26 December that Moore was able to set out to find out what had happened.

Gone without trace

When Moore reached the island, he discovered that the three lighthouse keepers had disappeared without trace. At first, he thought that they must have been swept away in stormy seas. There was **evidence** that a wave or waves about 30 metres (100 feet) high had swept across the island's **jetty**, and this could easily have drowned anyone outside the lighthouse.

The 'stormy seas' theory was proved wrong by the timing of events. The last entry in the chief keeper's log (record book) was for 9 a.m. on 15 December. The light had not been lit that night, although the lights were all fully stocked and in perfect order, so the three keepers had disappeared sometime between 9 a.m. and darkness on 15 December. And 15 December had been a calm day; the storms had not begun until 16 December, a day after the keepers had disappeared. The events leading to the keepers' disappearance were a complete mystery.

In the past, shepherds from the Hebrides brought their sheep to the island to feed on its rich grass. But they would never themselves spend the night there – for they said Eilean More was haunted by spirits. It began to seem that spirits must have taken the lighthousemen away.

A possible answer

The likely answer to the riddle of Eilean More was finally provided in 1947. A journalist named Iain Campbell visited the island on a calm day, and was standing near to the jetty. The sea suddenly heaved up in front of him, to a height of about 20 metres (65 feet), before sinking back down again. Campbell was sure that anyone standing on the jetty would have been drowned. It seems likely that a similar sea surge 46 years earlier must have claimed the lives of the three keepers.

Eilean More is the northernmost of the Flannan Islands, which lie off the west coast of Scotland.

Sea surges

What could have caused the sea surge that claimed the lives of the three lighthouse keepers?

Two main possibilities have been suggested. The first is that it was most likely to have been a giant wave. Waves travel across the ocean at different speeds and, sometimes, one large wave catches up to another and the two join their energy together, making a more powerful 'rogue' wave. The second possibility was that a freak combination of tides caused a sudden rise in sea level.

FILE CLOSED

On 26 November 1922, a group of men stood in a tunnel under the Egyptian desert. It had taken them years of searching to find this place, which they hoped would lead to the undisturbed tomb of the Egyptian **pharaoh**, Tutankhamen. Their hopes were fulfilled and the tomb was opened, but disaster was to be the outcome.

The men were led by the English **archaeologist** Howard Carter and the wealthy Lord Carnarvon. Carnarvon watched as Carter made a hole in a sealed doorway. Carter leant forwards, holding a candle, and peered through the hole.

'Can you see anything?' asked Carnarvon.
'Yes,' replied Carter, 'wonderful things.'

The archaeologists could not believe what they had discovered. The tomb was filled with an amazing array of treasures: golden coffins and other artefacts from thousands of years ago. But, within months, tragedy was to strike. Carnarvon was dead, and so were others who had been there when the tomb was opened. People began to suggest that they had fallen victim to the subject of an ancient legend: the Mummy's Curse.

Archaeologists and diggers look on as Tutankhamen's treasures are brought into the light.

The story of the Mummy's Curse began long before the day Howard Carter knocked a hole in the doorway of the pharaoh's tomb. The rulers of ancient Egypt were thought to be gods, and were buried with treasure in elaborate tombs. The treasures were incredibly valuable, and there were plenty of tomb robbers who tried to steal them after the burial places had been sealed.

A warning to thieves

To stop tomb raiders, the ancient Egyptians designed burial places with hidden chambers, false passageways and pretend doorways. They also sometimes placed a warning on the tomb, hoping that the curse of a dead pharaoh would be enough to stop people from trying to steal his treasures. Tutankhamen's tomb is supposed to have been cursed, 'Death shall come on swift wings to him who disturbs the peace of the King.' This warning cannot now be seen on the tomb.

Soon after Tutankhamen's tomb had been opened, his curse appeared to start its work. Lord Carnarvon became ill and was rushed to hospital in Cairo. Within days, he had died. Many reports say that, at that moment, all the lights in Cairo mysteriously went out; back home in England, Carnarvon's favourite dog howled and then dropped dead.

The true cause of Carnarvon's death is not certain. Most accounts say that he died because a mosquito bite on his cheek became infected. Some versions say that he cut the bite while shaving, which led to the infection. One story says that, when Tutankhamen's mummy was unwrapped, it had a cut on the cheek in exactly the same place.

A bad omen?

Legend says that Carter discovered Tutankhamen's tomb in mysterious circumstances. In 1922, he returned from a visit to England with a pet canary. His foreman, a man named Ahmed, saw the bird and exclaimed, 'A golden bird! It will lead us to the tomb.' Soon afterwards, Carter's men discovered a step cut into the rock; it was the first of sixteen steps that led to the doorway of the tomb. But when Carter returned home that night, his servant was holding a few yellow feathers. A cobra had come into the house and killed the canary. Cobras were an ancient symbol of the pharaohs, and the servant was convinced that the canary's death was a bad **omen**. He begged Carter not to disturb the tomb, but Carter refused to listen.

Further deaths

By 1929, eleven people had apparently fallen victim to the curse. But, by 1935, the newspapers claimed that there had been 21 victims, people who had died prematurely or in mysterious circumstances. But subsequent **analysis** of the **statistics** does not bear out talk of a curse. Herbert E. Winlock, of the Metropolitan Museum of Art in New York, estimates that there were 22 people present when the tomb was opened. By 1934, only six of them had died. Of those present at the opening of Tutankhamen's coffin in 1924, only two died in the next ten years. Of the ten people present when the mummy was unwrapped in 1925, all survived until at least 1934. These findings suggest that the Mummy's Curse was not as effective as some people have alleged.

Perhaps the best **evidence** that the curse does not exist is the story of Howard Carter, the man who actually broke into the tomb. Carter lived a fairly long life, and died of natural causes at the age of 65.

The Mummy's Curse promised that death would reach those who disturbed the tomb 'on swift wings'. Perhaps death missed its flight: figures suggest that, in fact, they lived to a ripe old age. Howard Carter himself would have been pleased with these statistics. He once said of the curse that 'all sane people should dismiss such inventions with contempt'.

Carter and Carnarvon stand in the partly destroyed entrance to Tutankhamen's burial chamber.

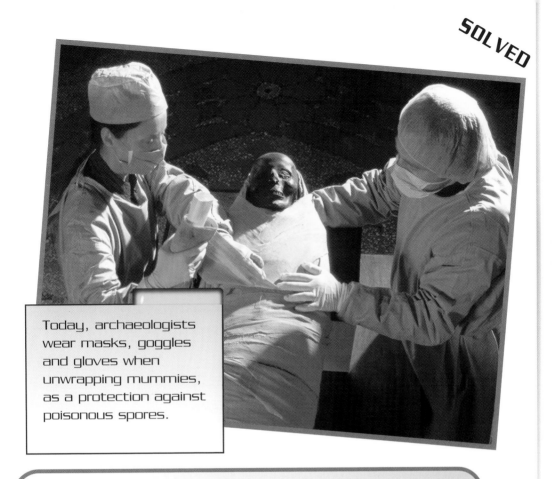

Today, archaeologists wear masks, goggles and gloves when unwrapping mummies, as a protection against poisonous spores.

Ancient spores

In 1999, a German microbiologist (scientist who studies micro-organisms) called Gotthard Kramer suggested a scientific **explanation** for the deaths resulting from the Mummy's Curse. His analysis of 40 mummies found that each carried several dangerously toxic (poisonous) mould **spores** that are capable of surviving for thousands of years.

Kramer thought that when the tombs were opened, incoming fresh air had possibly disturbed these spores and blown them up into the air, where they could be breathed in. Once inside a person's body, the poison they contain could lead to organ failure or even death. This is what may have happened to some of the archaeologists at the Tutankhamen site.

One evening in August 1977, Janet and Peter Harper complained to their mother that their beds were moving around as they lay on them. She came upstairs to investigate, but found that the beds were still. The next night, though, the children claimed to have heard a shuffling sound. When their mother came upstairs, she could hear nothing but, as she turned off the light, she, too, heard the noise. Suddenly, there were four loud knocks on the wall. Then a chest of drawers moved by itself. It was pushed back into position, but moved away again almost immediately. Terrified, Peggy Harper gathered up Janet, Peter and her two other children, and fled to her next-door neighbours' house. The Enfield **Poltergeist** had arrived.

Strange knockings

A poltergeist is supposedly a noisy, mischievous spirit that delights in moving furniture and throwing things around, and usually hangs around children who are approaching **puberty**. The Enfield Poltergeist, once it had made its presence known, lost no time in starting on some typical poltergeist activity. Peggy Harper and her neighbours came back to the house to investigate, and heard the strange knocking on the walls once more. They decided to call the police, who arrived some time after 11 p.m. The knocking continued, and one policeman apparently saw a chair move across the floor under its own power.

Marbles and bricks

From this point onwards, the events at the Harper house in North London became more serious. For the next three days, a storm of small plastic bricks and marbles were flung around, and then Janet began to speak in a strange, gravelly man's voice.

Bill's voice

The voice spoken by Janet claimed to have several identities: the clearest was 'Bill', who said that he was the ghost of someone who had died in the house. It was later discovered that someone called Bill had, indeed, died in the house. No one could understand how such a deep voice could

Janet Harper, who seems to be in the grip of the Enfield poltergeist, is held to stop her harming herself.

Mysterious voices

Janet Harper's mysterious deep voice, which claimed to be the voice of a spirit named 'Bill', was investigated by speech therapists.

We all have vocal cords to enable us to speak, but the speech therapists suspected that Janet had learnt to use a second set of vocal cords. Very few people ever learn to use these, although actors sometimes use these 'false cords' to speak in a deep, gravelly voice.

A recording of 'Bill's' voice was analysed on a **larynograph**, a machine that measures the frequency of a person's voice as it passes through the larynx. The **analysis** suggested that Janet was indeed using her 'false cords' to speak as 'Bill'. However, using these 'false cords' usually has an effect on a person's normal voice. Oddly, no changes were noticed in Janet's voice after 'Bill' had been speaking.

Further investigations

At the suggestion of the reporter from the *Daily Mirror* who was covering the Enfield Poltergeist, the Harpers asked for help from the Society for Psychical Research (SPR). The SPR sent **investigator** Maurice Grosse to stay with the Harpers in an attempt to find out what was happening.

An unseen hand

For the first few days, nothing happened. Then, on about the fourth night, a loud crash announced that the poltergeist was back. A chair had apparently flung itself across Janet's room. Grosse was hit by a marble thrown by what he called an 'unseen hand', and events began to escalate.

People felt their bedclothes being whipped off the bed in the middle of the night. Fires started and suddenly went out, strange pools of water began to appear on the floor and pieces of metal would bend or snap mysteriously. Most worrying of all, photos taken at the time show Janet being picked up and thrown from her bed.

Hospital tests

Janet was taken to Maudsley Hospital in South London for tests, to check whether she was physically or mentally abnormal in some way.

Janet apparently being flung from her bed by the poltergeist.

No problems were found but, while Janet was away, the Enfield Poltergeist stopped its activities. **Investigators** began to suspect that Janet might be behind the strange events. Then, suddenly, after two years of mysterious events, the Enfield Poltergeist disappeared – and was never heard from again.

Weighing the evidence

No definite conclusion has been reached about whether the Enfield Poltergeist was a genuine **supernatural** event or a **hoax**. In the end, people have to weigh the **evidence** for themselves before making a decision:

Evidence against:

1. Forensic evidence suggested that Janet had taught herself to speak in a deep voice.

2. The Harpers, a family of five, were living in a three-bedroomed house. At the time, many people made up haunted house stories as a way of getting the council to move them to a bigger home.

3. Janet was caught on a hidden camera bending spoons and trying to bend a metal pipe.

4. Janet was very athletic, and loved pulling tricks on strangers. This might explain how she was able to fling herself out of bed.

Evidence for:

1. No changes happened to her normal voice, as would usually happen when using 'false cords'.

2. Mrs Harper had not applied to move house, and, even during the poltergeist activities, she refused to leave her home.

3. Janet claimed that she did this to see if the **investigators** could tell the difference between a real poltergeist event and a hoax. She said that they always caught her when she tried to con them.

4. Just because Janet could have flung herself out of bed does not mean that she did.

One night in 1988, a group of men was driving past the town of Wittlich, in Germany. One of them noticed that the candle that traditionally burned in a shrine by the roadside had gone out. Local legend said that the candle kept away a werewolf that had once terrorized the town.

Later that night, something was heard attacking the fence of a military airfield. The men who went to investigate were terrified to see a giant wolf-like creature stand on its back legs and leap over the 3 metre (10 foot) fence. Their attack dogs refused to follow the creature and, instead, stood quivering by the fence. Had the werewolf returned?

An ancient Greek werewolf

The idea of a human who can turn into a wolf-like creature, ready to rip open the throats of innocent victims, is not a new one. Humans have feared werewolves for centuries. More than 2500 years ago, the ancient Greeks wrote of men who became wolves: Damarchus of Arcadia, who won a boxing gold medal at the Olympics in about 400 BC, was said to be a werewolf. The word 'werewulf' was probably first used in English in 1020.

A German werewolf being hunted in 17...

Werewolves in the Middle Ages

Werewolves first became really popular – or rather, unpopular – in Europe towards the end of the Middle Ages. They were seen as agents of the Devil, and were often mentioned in **witchcraft** trials. In 1521, for example, the 'werewolves' of Poligny, France were burnt to death as a punishment for their apparently ungodly ways. Between 1520 and 1630 there were more than 30,000 werewolf trials in France alone. Hundreds of people died having been convicted of being werewolves.

The idea of there being 30,000 werewolves wandering around the medieval French countryside now seems preposterous. But there is **evidence** that werewolves of some sort – people who at least believed that they were a wolf in human form – have always existed. Some may even walk among us today.

Lycanthropic drugs

Lycanthropy is a condition in which the sufferer believes that they are a wolf or other fierce animal. In Europe during the 1500s and 1600s, there were thousands of reports of werewolves. Today, scientists have discovered two possible **explanations** for people imagining themselves to be **supernatural** in this way:

1. Some accounts say that humans used 'magic salve' to turn themselves into werewolves. This may have been a strong drug similar to **LSD**, which allowed them to imagine that strange events were taking place. LSD is a **hallucinogenic** drug: people who have taken it may see **visions** of things that are not there, and imagine their bodies to be changing shape when, in reality, they are not.

2. The 'werewolves' were actually suffering from ergot poisoning. Ergot also has hallucinogenic effects.

Delusions and reality

No one has ever captured a 'real' werewolf – a human who can take the shape of a wolf – alive or dead. But there are scientifically investigated examples of people who thought that they were werewolves. These are people suffering from a rare **psychological** disorder called lycanthropy. An article in the *American Journal of Psychiatry* described this as 'a **psychosis** [severe mental illness] in which the patient has **delusions** of being a wild animal (usually a wolf)'. A human who imagines he or she is a wolf can be every bit as dangerous as an actual wolf, so this is a serious condition.

Growling and snarling

One case from the 1970s involved a woman who thought she was 'an animal with claws'. She came to the attention of the authorities because one night she had sat up in bed and started growling, scratching herself and anyone near her, and chewing at the bed. She claimed that the Devil had come into her body and turned her into an animal. The woman was admitted to hospital, where she told doctors that when she looked into the mirror she saw 'the head of a wolf in place of a face on my own body – just a long-nosed wolf with teeth, groaning, snarling, growling'. No one else could see any physical change in her at this time.

The woman was treated with drugs and counselling, and within ten weeks had been released from hospital. The doctors who treated her felt that she had been suffering from a rare form of schizophrenia (a mental illness). When they investigated other modern 'werewolves', the doctors felt that these people, too, had been suffering from the same kind of mental illness.

Psychiatrists such as this one may, very rarely, have to help people who believe themselves to be werewolves.

A lack of evidence

Where does all this leave the Wittlich werewolf? Probably nowhere; there is very little **evidence** that it ever really existed. The story appears on several Internet sites, but all the witnesses seem to have disappeared. No one has any photos of the ground the werewolf walked on; there are no wolf-like footprints to show its presence. This kind of werewolf – the kind of werewolf that appears in fairy tales and stories – does not exist. It is the other kind, the kind that lives in people's heads, that is real.

The 'werewolves' of Zacatecas

The Fajardo Aceves family lives in Zacatecas, Mexico. The family live in isolation, shunned by the local people, and do not mix with outsiders. The reasons?

- Each member of the family is covered in fur-like hair that grows all over their body.

- The 'fur' grows even on the faces of the women and girls, and makes the family look just like classic Hollywood werewolves.

- The disorder is caused by a rare **genetic** disorder, for which there is no cure.

It may be that people who looked like the Fajardo Aceves family first gave rise to the idea that humans can become wolves. Of course, the members of this family are human beings, not wolves.

Jesús Manuel Fajardo Aceves, a member of the Fajardo Aceves family from Mexico.

Solve it!

This story comes from the Ille de Noirmoutier in western France, in the winter of 1618. One morning, just after eating a breakfast of bread and cheese, Julienne Laporte, the daughter of a poor labourer, suddenly became ill. She seemed to be seeing things that no one else could see, and would snatch at the air as if trying to swat away invisible creatures that were buzzing around her head. Then she began to twitch all over, and to writhe around in her bed shouting.

Possessed by the Devil

The local doctor was summoned, as was the priest. The doctor could not explain the symptoms, but the priest thought that he could. Julienne was clearly possessed by the Devil; he had heard of such cases before, and read about them in religious texts. The key issue now, said the priest, was to find out the identity of the witch who had cursed the poor girl.

By this time, Julienne had recovered slightly, and was able to talk to her father. He reported that, the night before, she had had an argument with an old woman called Véronique Delmaso, who lived nearby. She had asked Julienne and her friend to stop making so much noise outside her house. When they refused, Delmaso spat at their feet and walked indoors, muttering curses. There was still more **evidence**. Julienne said that, while she had been unconscious, the old woman had visited her in her dreams.

A young woman accused of witchcraft tries to defend herself.

The case seemed clear. There had been several **accusations** of **witchcraft** on Ille de Noirmoutier and, only three months before, two witches had been burned in the city of Angers. Véronique Delmaso was clearly a witch, who had used **supernatural** means to punish a young girl for her lack of charity. She was arrested and taken away by the authorities. After a short trial she was burned to death, having finally admitted her crime while being tortured.

Was Véronique Delmaso a witch?

Was Véronique Delmaso really a witch? And, if not, what really happened to Julienne Laporte? Here are some questions you could ask as you try to work out the answer:

1 What were Julienne's symptoms?
2 Could these symptoms have been caused by anything other than witchcraft?
3 Was Julienne from a wealthy background or a poor one?
4 Had Julienne eaten or drunk anything that day that might have affected her?
5 Is there any actual evidence linking her illness to the old woman Véronique Delmaso?

ANSWERS
1 She seems to have had **delusions** and **convulsions**, as well as a fever.
2 Yes, they could have been caused by a drug.
3 Her father was a labourer, so she was from a poor background.
4 She had eaten some cheese and a piece of bread.
5 No, there is no evidence except that they met the day before. Even then, there was no physical contact between them.

Glossary

accuse to say that someone has done something wrong

adopted taken into a new relationship. The word is especially used to describe children who have new parents who are not their birth parents.

afflicted to suffer from an illness or something horrible

analysis separation of something into the parts that make it up to investigate what it is made of

archaeologist person who studies human history by digging up the places where people once lived, then examining what is found there

cairn cone-shaped pile of small rocks or stones. Cairns are often used to mark the summits of mountains or to indicate a path.

cloven hoof cloven means split or divided, and a hoof is the hard, nail-like area at the end of some animals' legs. Cloven-hoofed animals include sheep, goats and oxen. The Christian Devil is said to be cloven-hoofed.

convulsions series of violent physical movements that cannot be controlled by the sufferer

decompose decay or rot

delusions false beliefs or impressions; for example, someone who thinks they have the head of a wolf is very likely to be suffering from a delusion.

DNA type of molecule in the form of a twisted double strand (double helix) found in every cell of every living thing. It carries genetic information, which determines an organism's characteristics.

evidence proof of an idea about how something works or has happened

exorcize expel an evil spirit from the place or person it has occupied. Exorcisms are usually performed by Christian priests, who believe they can use the power of God to expel evil spirits that work for the Devil.

explanation answer to why certain things happen, or why people do certain things

fasting going without food, and sometimes drink. Fasting is especially associated with religion, where people sometimes use fasting as a way of showing their devotion to God.

forensic pathologist scientist who studies the causes of diseases and injuries, and then delivers their findings to the courts, police or other authorities

Gaelic language spoken in Ireland and Scotland, and some small islands off the west coast of Britain. Began to die out in the early 20th century, but is now spoken more often.

genetic relating to the genes, the basic units consisting of a sequence of DNA that transmits characteristics from one generation to the next

hallucinogenic substance that causes people to imagine they see things that are not there

hoax attempt to fool a person or people, usually to get money or something from them

hysteria uncontrollable wild behaviour

investigation formal inquiry to find out as much information as possible about something

investigator person who tries to discover the truth about an event

jetty platform sticking out into the sea or a river, used to load and unload boats

Kirlian photography type of photography that uses an electrical charge to generate an image of energy surrounding the living thing being photographed

LSD abbreviation of 'lysergic acid diethylamide'. LSD was one of the first hallucinogenic drugs.

magnetic field area around a magnetic object within which its magnetic force can be felt

magistrate person who is not an appointed judge but an ordinary citizen who makes legal judgements for the local community

massacre many people being killed at one time

mountaineer person who climbs mountains

omen something that happens that is thought to show that an important good or evil event is about to occur

petrified paralysed (struck motionless) with fear or astonishment

pharaoh ruler of ancient Egypt, who was thought to be a king and god at the same time

poltergeist kind of mischievous and sometimes violent ghost. Poltergeists are said to knock on walls, move furniture around and throw things about the room.

psychological relating to the science of the mind

psychosis severe mental illness, which usually results in the sufferer imagining strange and frightening things (such as voices giving instructions), and being unable to live a normal life

puberty stage of growth in young people. During puberty, the body undergoes many changes in preparation for eventual sexual reproduction.

spectre form of a witch, visible only to the witch's victim

spore single cell that is capable of flourishing and growing into a more complex creature

statistics numerical facts

summit top of a hill or mountain

supernatural defying explanation by the laws of science

trance sleep-like state in which the sufferer does not respond well, or at all, to things happening around them

vision seeing something that others cannot see, brought on by imagination or religious experience

voice analysis scientific study of the voice, to prove exactly who was speaking

witchcraft magic performed by witches, usually thought of as doing harm

witness someone who sees something happen. Witnesses are often asked to give evidence at a trial.

Get into forensics

Supernatural investigation of any kind is a complex and fascinating business. **Investigators** working in various fields may be called upon to explain a past event or an ongoing situation that seems, at first, to be beyond explanation. Using scientific methods and specialized equipment, investigators record and analyse all the information gathered. Sometimes, answers present themselves quite easily but, occasionally, years go by before any firm conclusions can be reached – if ever.

Like supernatural investigators, criminal scientific investigators, known as forensic investigators, have to analyse **evidence**. They may need to make identifications from **DNA** fragments, check photographs for fakes, examine paper fibres under an electron microscope, find the age of ancient bones using radiocarbon dating or match tyre tracks.

One person alone cannot master such a wide range of skills, and those involved in forensic investigations often perform highly specialized tasks. Ballistics experts, for example, will match projectiles with weapons and detect traces of explosives on fabric or skin. Toxicologists may be called on by a **forensic pathologist** carrying out a post-mortem (after death) examination to look at a particular organ for indications of a hard-to-detect poison.

In fact, the range of skills required is so broad that it covers almost every aspect of science and medicine: physics, chemistry and biology, medicine and dentistry, anthropology, archaeology and psychology. So any reader wanting to pursue a career in this area will need to begin with some scientific qualifications.

Useful websites

The Salem Witch Museum website has accounts of the trials, responses to FAQs and a virtual tour:
> www.salemwitchmuseum.com

The story of the discovery of Tutankhamun's tomb, including information about the potentially fatal **spores** found in mummies:
> www.unmuseum.org/mummy.htm

An excellent source for debunking (disproving) the modern vampire myth. It includes the account of the original investigation of the death of Peter Plogojowitz:
> www.csicop.org

The home site of the *Fortean Times* magazine:
> www.forteantimes.com

A science site that carries a regular weekly article explaining the science behind recent headlines:
> www.whyfiles.org

Hundreds of articles and web pages about all kinds of popular science topics:
> www.pbs.org/wgbh/nova/

Further reading

An Encyclopedia of Claims, Frauds, and Hoaxes of the Occult and Supernatural, James Randi (St Martin's Griffin, 1995)

Egyptian Mummies, Bob Brier (Caxton Editions, 2001)

Salem-Village Witchcraft: A Documentary Record of Local Conflict in Colonial New England, eds. Paul Boyer and Stephen Nissenbaum (Northeastern University Press, 1993)

The Mummy: A Handbook of Egyptian Funerary Archaeology, E. A. Wallis Budge (Dover Publications, 1989)

The Vampire Encyclopedia, Matthew Bunson (Gramercy Books, 2000)

This House is Haunted: Investigation of the Enfield Poltergeist, Guy Lyon Playfair (Souvenir Press, 1980)

Vampires, Werewolves and Demons, Lynn Myring (Usborne, 1992)

Index

Titles in the *Forensic Files* series include:

Hardback   0 431 16020 1

Hardback   0 431 16021 X

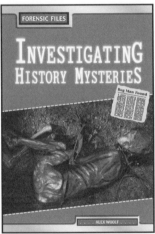

Hardback   0 431 16022 8

Hardback   0 431 16023 6

Hardback   0 431 16024 4

Hardback   0 431 16025 2

Find out about the other titles in this series on our website www.heinemann.co.uk/library